First Facts

Spiders

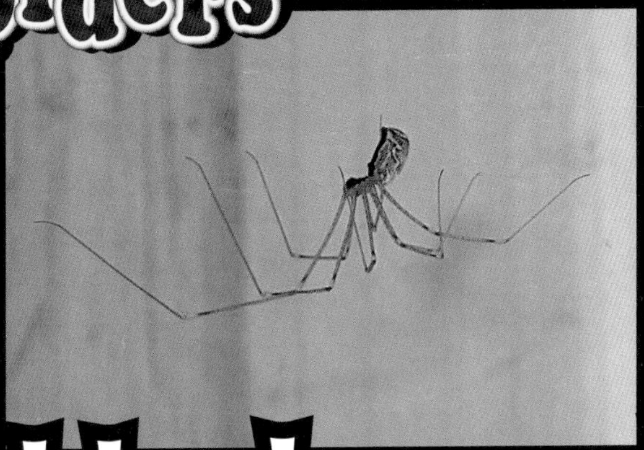

Daddy Long-Leg Spiders

by Molly Kolpin

Consultant:
Pedro Barbosa, PhD
Department of Entomology
University of Maryland, College Park

CAPSTONE PRESS
a capstone imprint

First Facts is published by Capstone Press,
151 Good Counsel Drive, P.O. Box 669, Mankato, Minnesota 56002.
www.capstonepub.com

 Books published by Capstone Press are manufactured with paper
containing at least 10 percent post-consumer waste.

Library of Congress Cataloging-in-Publication Data
Kolpin, Molly.
  Daddy long-leg spiders / Molly Kolpin.
    p. cm.—(First Facts. Spiders)
  Includes bibliographical references and index.
  Summary: "A brief introduction to daddy long-leg spiders, including their habitat,
food, and life cycle"—Provided by publisher.
  ISBN 978-1-4296-5390-9 (library binding)
  1. Pholcidae—Juvenile literature. I. Title. II. Series.
  QL458.42.P4K67 2011
    595.4'4—dc22   2010027822

Editorial Credits
Lori Shores, editor; Kyle Grenz, designer; Eric Gohl, media researcher; Laura Manthe,
     production specialist

Photo Credits
123RF/Antonio Veraldi, 15; mfelixphoto, 1
Alamy/Michael Hampson, 7
iStockphoto/James Benet, cover
Nature Picture Library/Premaphotos, 13; Stephen Dalton, 9, 20
Newscom, 16
Pete Carmichael, 19, 21
Shutter Point/Jami Mattice, 5
Shutterstock/R.S.Jegg, 10

Essential content terms are **bold** and are defined at the bottom
of the page where they first appear.

Printed in the United States of America in Melrose Park, Illinois.
092010   005935LKS11

Table of Contents

Standing Tall

Daddy long-leg spiders are famous for their extra-long legs. These **arachnids** are less than 0.5 inch (1.3 centimeters) long. But their eight legs can be 25 times longer than their bodies.

Spider Fact!

Some daddy long-leg spiders have six eyes. Others have eight eyes.

arachnid—an animal with four pairs of legs and no backbone, wings, or antennae

5

Spider Bodies

Like all spiders, daddy long-leg spiders have two main body parts. Their bodies are gray or brown. Some daddy long-leg spiders have dark bands of color on their bodies.

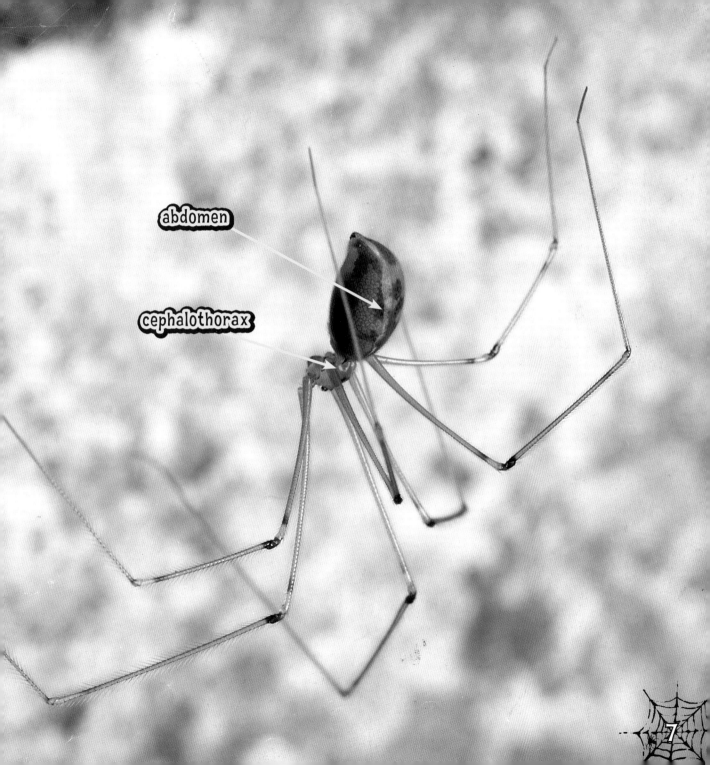

abdomen

cephalothorax

7

Basement Neighbors

Daddy long-leg spiders are found everywhere except Antarctica. They live in dry deserts and cold, wet areas. But they are most common in the **tropics**.

where daddy long-leg spiders live

North America

Europe

Asia

Africa

South America

Australia

Antarctica

N W E S

tropics—the extremely hot area of Earth near the equator

web

Daddy long-leg spiders build webs in dark areas such as caves or under rocks. They also live in attics and dark basement corners.

Spider Fact!

A daddy long-leg spider's jaws aren't strong enough to bite through human skin.

Fast Attack

A daddy long-leg spider eats small flies, ants, and moths. The spider waits for **prey** in its web. When a bug wanders into the web, the spider jumps into action.

The spider bites its prey and quickly wraps it up. **Venom** from the spider's bite kills the prey and turns the body to liquid. Then the spider sucks up the mushy meal.

prey—an animal hunted by another animal for food
venom—a harmful liquid made by some animals

11

Spider Versus Spider

Sometimes a daddy long-leg spider goes hunting for food. It taps a leg on another spider's web. The spider rushes out of hiding to see what is in the web. But the daddy long-leg is ready for battle. It bites the spider and gobbles it up.

13

Break a Leg

Frogs, lizards, and birds eat daddy long-leg spiders. To get away from a **predator**, a daddy long-leg spider breaks off one of its legs. The predator grabs the leg while the spider runs away.

Spider Fact!

Young daddy long-leg spiders can grow new legs to replace broken ones.

predator—an animal that hunts other animals for food

silk

spinneret

Spider Fact!

A daddy long-leg spider's silk isn't sticky. But prey and predators get stuck in the tangled threads.

Superhero Silk

Sometimes daddy long-leg spiders trap enemies with **silk**. When an enemy comes close, the spider pulls silk from its **spinneret**. It throws the silk around the predator's body. The predator is stuck, and the spider gets away.

silk—a string made by spiders
spinneret—a body part used to make silk thread

Baby Long-legs

Male and female daddy long-leg spiders mate year-round. The female lays about 20 eggs at a time. She wraps the eggs in an **egg sac** that she carries in her mouth. The baby spiders, called **spiderlings**, hatch from the eggs in two to three weeks.

egg sac—a small pouch made of silk that holds spider eggs
spiderling—a young spider

Life Cycle of a Daddy Long-leg Spider

Newborn

Spiderlings hang from their mother's face for one to two weeks.

spiderling

eggs

Young

As they grow, daddy long-leg spiders shed their outer skeletons.

Adult

Female daddy long-leg spiders live for three years. Males live for only one year.

Many Names

Daddy long-leg spiders are known by many names. Because they live in basements, people call them cellar spiders. They're also called granddaddy long-legs or daddy long-leggers.

Amazing but True!

If a daddy long-leg spider is trapped by a predator, it has one last trick. The spider shakes so quickly that it becomes an almost invisible blur. The predator becomes confused and doesn't know where to strike!

Glossary

arachnid (uh-RACK-nid)—an animal with four pairs of legs and no backbone, wings, or antennae

egg sac (EG SAK)—a small pouch made of silk that holds spider eggs

predator (PRED-uh-tur)—an animal that hunts other animals for food

prey (PRAY)—an animal hunted by another animal for food

silk (SILK)—a string made by spiders

spiderling (SPYE-dur-ling)—a young spider

spinneret (spin-nuh-RET)—a body part used to make silk thread

tropics (TROP-iks)—the extremely hot area of Earth near the equator

venom (VEN-uhm)—a harmful liquid produced by some animals

Read More

Anderson, Catherine. *Daddy Longlegs.* Bug Books. Chicago: Heinemann Library, 2008.

Bishop, Nic. *Spiders.* New York: Scholastic Nonfiction, 2007.

René, Ellen. *Investigating Spiders and Their Webs.* Science Detectives. New York: PowerKids Press, 2009.

Internet Sites

FactHound offers a safe, fun way to find Internet sites related to this book. All of the sites on FactHound have been researched by our staff.

Here's all you do:

Visit *www.facthound.com*

Type in this code: 9781429653909

Check out projects, games and lots more at
www.capstonekids.com

23

Index